THE WARNING LABEL BOOK

WARNING:

by Joey Green, Tim Nyberg, and Tony Dierckins

Martin's Griffin ⚏ New York

Warning: Manufacturers, after receiving additional warnings from their legal departments, sometimes delete, revise, or amend the warning labels on their products. The legal department at our publishing house demanded that we warn you that the warnings in this warning-label book were found prior to the publication of this book and may or may not be found on current packaging or labeling. Similarly, please be warned that this book does not, to the best of our knowledge, contain any warnings that have come into existence after this book was printed.

Library of Congress Cataloging-in-Publication Data

Green, Joey.
    The warning label book / by Joey Green, Tim Nyberg, and Tony Dierckins. — 1st ed.
        p.   cm.
    ISBN 0-312-19534-6 (alk. paper)
    1. Warning labels—Humor.   2. American wit and humor.   I. Nyberg, Tim.   II. Dierckins, Tony.
    III. Title.
    PN6231.W29G74   1998
    818'.5402—dc21   98-24108
                                                                      CIP

First St. Martin's Griffin Edition: November 1998

10 9 8 7 6

CAUTION: Dedication

WARNING:

This book is dedicated to the lawyers who write blatantly obvious warnings on products. Keep up the good work.

CAUTION: Introduction

Warnings. They're everywhere. On toys. On hair dryers. On compact discs. On fast-food coffee cups. Almost everything for sale today comes with a warning. Why?

Two reasons:

1. Some idiot used the product improperly and ended up in the emergency room.

2. That same idiot knew an ambulance-chasing attorney who figured they could sue the manufacturer for some major loot.

Now, most of us have enough common sense not to take a bath with an electric blender, but thanks to all this senseless litigation, products now come with warnings that treat us all like a bunch of slack-jawed yokels. And frankly, we're sick of it.

So we've collected some of the more ridiculous warning labels on today's products along with a few outlandish stories that have spawned even more outlandish warnings. Plus, we've also thrown in dozens of handy warning stickers that you can slap on products you use every day. Enjoy the book, but be forewarned: Laughter is the best medicine, so do not read this book while driving a car or operating heavy machinery.

— The Authors

WARNING: Don't do anything stupid with this book and then try to sue us. You have been warned.

Found on the instruction sheet of a Conair Pro Style 1600 hair dryer:

WARNING: Do not use in shower. Never use while sleeping.

*And **never** blow-dry your hair while you're sleeping in the shower.*

Found on a microwave package of Orville Redenbacher's gourmet popping corn:

Do not puncture or tear bag before popping.

C'mon, Orville—you're taking all the fun out of watching corn pop.

Found on a package of Ray-O-Vac Renewal AA reusable batteries:

If swallowed or lodged in ear or nose see doctor.

*If you lodge a battery in your ear or nose, you might also
want to see a psychiatrist or consider a career in the circus.*

How ya supposed to read the label when the battery is stuck in your nose?

MR. BRILLIANT SEZ

WARNING: Page 3

Found on Axius Sno-Off Automobile Windshield cover:

CAUTION: Never drive with the cover on your windshield.

Unless, of course, you cut a big hole in it so you can see.

FDA proposed warning label for packages of Frito-Lay's new Max potato chips, made with Olestra fat substitute:

> This product contains Olestra. Olestra may cause abdominal cramping and loose stools. Olestra inhibits the absorption of some vitamins and other nutrients. Vitamins A, D, E and K have been added.

Factoid: Procter & Gamble Inc. has reportedly asked the Food and Drug Administration to allow use of a less-graphic warning label because consumer test groups reacted negatively to the proposed FDA warning. No doubt they had problems finding a consumer group that would react positively to such a warning.

It's a potato chip!
No, it's a laxative!
No, it's a multivitamin!

Instructions found on almost all bottles of shampoo:

Wet hair. Lather. Rinse. Repeat.

If you follow these instructions literally, you'll spend the rest of your life shampooing your hair.

WARNING: Page 6

Found on Super Tiger Champagne Party Popper (small plastic novelty bottles that shower confetti after a string is pulled):

WARNING: Flammable.

Yet the other side of the label reads:

Flameproof—contains 0.25 grains of powder or less.

Novelty fireworks can be dangerous enough. Fireworks manufactured by companies who hire schizophrenic warning label writers, well, that's just plain disturbing.

Found on a bottle containing a purified chemical:

> For purposes of complying with the New Jersey Right to Know Act, contents partially unknown.

*Who in the name of—
oh, it's a New Jersey law.
Never mind.*

Found on Tilex mildew remover:

Use only in well-ventilated areas.

If you were in a well-ventilated area in the first place, why would there be mildew?

Found on packages of Betty Crocker Fruit Roll-Ups:

Peel fruit from cellophane before eating.

If consumers can't tell the difference between your product and its packaging, you might consider adding more fruit flavor.

Found on a Bungee cord:

USE EXTREME CAUTION when stretching cord over load. Keep face and other vulnerable body parts away from potential cord rebound path.

But feel free to attach the Bungee cord to yourself and leap off a tall bridge.

Found on Tootsietoy Marshall eight-shot ring cap pistol:

> **WARNING:** Do not fire more than four ring caps consecutively.
> Do not carry ring caps in your pockets.

This warning raises several questions. If you aren't supposed to fire more than four ring caps at a time, why is this cap gun an eight-shooter? Where are you supposed to carry ring caps if not in your pocket? And more important, why buy your kid a toy gun in the first place?

Found on many return envelopes:

Post Office will not deliver mail without postage.

*Was there ever a time
when the post office did
deliver mail without postage?*

Found on a box of Tampax tampons:

Remove used tampon before inserting a new one.

Well now, that might explain the irritability associated with the use of this product.

No wonder my wife feels so bloated all the time.

MR. BRILLIANT SEZ

Found on the inside of a pull-top lid of liquid radiator sealant:

CAUTION: Do not lick lid.

Yeah, but after drinking the entire bottle of radiator sealant, it's hard to contain ourselves.

The McDonald's Coffee Story

One day, Stella Liebeck pulled up to the drive-through window at a McDonald's restaurant and ordered a cup of coffee. She accidentally spilled the coffee on herself and suffered severe burns. She sued McDonald's.

In 1994, a jury awarded Liebeck approximately $2.7 million. The case sent shock waves across America. How could McDonald's possibly be held liable? Any idiot knows that if you spill a hot cup of coffee on yourself, you'll get burned, right? The fact is, McDonald's had been selling scalding hot coffee for years. The fast-food chain had been warned repeatedly to stop serving its coffee piping hot. The jury was, in a sense, penalizing McDonald's for years of neglect.

Since that case, every cup of coffee served at McDonald's comes with the warning:

WARNING: Bonus Section

The case stunned corporate America. The slightest possibility of a financially crippling liability suit terrified highly paid corporate attorneys who earn their pay protecting the coffers of America's manufacturers. So, to cover their corporate backsides, the lawyers slapped warnings on any and every product their companies made—to the point of absurdity.

But here's a little something few people know about the case. Following a settlement, Liebeck's award was cut to less than $600,000. She didn't even get a free cup of coffee out of the deal.

And that's . . . the rest of the story.

Found on a box of Kellogg's Pop-Tarts:

WARNING: Pastry filling may be hot when heated.

*Wow! Free physics lesson
with every box!*

Found on a can of Salon Selectives hair-styling mousse:

> **WARNING:** FLAMMABLE. Avoid fire, flame, or smoking during use and until hair is thoroughly dry.

Once hair is dry, return to your normal routine of setting fire to your head.

Found on *Batman: The Animated Series* Armor Set Halloween costume box:

PARENT: Please exercise caution—
mask and chest plate are not protective;
cape does not enable wearer to fly.

*Parent: If your child
believes that a polyester
sheet enables flight, you
should probably examine
that Halloween candy
more closely.*

WARNING: Page 20

Found on public rest room Continuous Roll Towel dispensers:

> **MAINTENANCE OPERATOR:** Failure to follow loading instructions could result in serious injury or death.

Death for failing to follow instructions? Who'd have thought that janitors were working under such strict scrutiny? What's the penalty for failing to fill all the toilet-paper holders?

Found on a box of Q-Tips cotton swabs:

> **WARNING:** Use only as directed. Entering the ear canal could cause injury. Keep out of reach of children.

Good warning. We don't see how anyone could possibly fit into an ear canal without hurting themselves, and if you did manage to shrink that small, you certainly wouldn't want any children reaching at you.

If we're not supposed to put them in our ears, what are they for?

MR. BRILLIANT SEZ

Found on a package of Equal sweetener with NutraSweet Tablet dispenser:

**If Tablets do not dispense, shake container and try again.
Do not use foreign objects to dislodge the Tablets,
or injury may result.**

---

*And whatever you do,
don't try to dislodge the tablets with a Q-Tip.*

Found in instructions for a computer mouse:

> **Do not dangle the mouse by its cable or throw mouse at co-workers.**

They're right. That short cable prevents the mouse from hitting co-workers from across the room. Try chucking a coffee cup or, better yet, a paperweight. Much more effective.

WARNING: Page 24

Found on an Intex brand Sno-Tube floatation toy:

Only to be used in water in which child is within its
depth and under supervision.

*Check label on child to verify
its appropriate depth.*

Sticker found on the base of a Bell Phones 900 megahertz cordless telephone:

> **Need help? Call (800) 800-8990 between**
> **8 AM — 4:30 PM PST**

*If your phone isn't working,
how are you supposed
to call the help line?*

WARNING: Page 26

Found on a can of Nabisco Easy Cheese:

For best results, remove cap.

For worst results, hit product repeatedly with a four-pound sledgehammer.

Found in specifications for a fire alarm system:

> There shall be three (3) access levels with level 4 being the highest level.

These instructions are flawed for two reasons: 1. Numeric inconsistency, B. The reader shall have to reread the instructions three times and won't understand them until the fourth time, and III. The instructions neglect to mention level 5.

Makes sense to me, but I used to work for the IRS.

MR. BRILLIANT SEZ

Found on plastic bags containing an *Anastasia* toy in Burger King Kids Club meals:

> This bag is not a toy. Please discard.

Forget the toy—the movie should have the warning:

> Like *Pocahontas*, this movie is historically inaccurate hooey designed to sell cheap plastic trinkets. Please disregard its contents.

Found on a box of GLAD drawstring cat-box liners:

WARNING: Not recommended for food storage.

Most dogs would disagree with that warning.

Yeah, but is it a toy?

MR. BRILLIANT SEZ

From a canister of Daptex latex foam sealant:

Ingestion may cause dizziness, headache, or nausea.

*Besides, foam sealant also
sticks to the roof of your
mouth.*

CAUTION: Bonus Section
Cigarette Warning Labels

Everyone is familiar with the U.S. Surgeon General's warnings on cigarette packs. Despite the warnings, people continue to smoke. Perhaps more would quit smoking—or never start—if these warning labels made stronger statements like:

> **WARNING:** Smoking makes your teeth yellow, your breath stink, your hair smell, and it stains your fingers brown. Good luck getting a date, or a job, you sniveling loser.

WARNING: Smoking is an expensive habit. If you start smoking when you are 18 years old and smoke one pack a day at the average cost of $2.50 a pack, you will spend $42,887.50 dollars on smoking by the time you retire at age 65—if you don't die of lung cancer before then—and that doesn't include the $150,000 for chemotherapy and another $260,000 for radiation.

WARNING: Smoking is an oral fixation stemming from a deeply buried subconscious conflict resulting from an unresolved childhood trauma. By lighting up, you are displaying your pathetic lack of self-esteem. What do you think Freud would say about you?

Found on Snak Club Gummy Worms:

No cholesterol, no preservatives. A meal in itself.

Why cook dinner when you can just give the kids a bagful of nutritious gummy worms?

Found on the back of a Tamagotchi virtual pet:

> **CAUTION:** Battery harmful or fatal if swallowed.

If you're smart enough to use a precision miniature Phillips screwdriver to remove the small plastic back panel to get to the battery, you probably already know better than to swallow it. On the other hand, all that work might make you hungry.

Does that mean it's okay to swallow the Tamagotchi if you take out the battery first?

MR. BRILLIANT SEZ

Found in the instructions for NAPA automotive fan belts:

CAUTION: Before starting service work,
be sure engine is off.

*A warning for people who
also hate stopping the car
to change a flat tire.*

Found on the safety booklet published for Cayman Airlines:

> If you are seated in an exit aisle and are unable to read this, please ask a stewardess to reseat you.

How would finding another seat suddenly enable you to read?

Found on packages containing Silly Putty:

WARNING: Not for use as earplugs.

Yeah, you don't want your kids eating anything that's been in someone's ears.

Found in a television set's owner's manual:

Do not pour liquids into your television set.

*And please don't use your
VCR as a toaster.*

Found on a package of Sea Salt, a.k.a Certified A.C.S. Crystal (described as "Sodium Chloride," which is, of course, salt):

CAUTION! May cause irritation. Ingestion of large amounts may cause systemic toxicity.

Wow! Pass the chips!

Found on instructions for a Bic cigarette lighter:

> **WARNING:** Ignite lighter away from face
> and clothing.

The ultimate stop-smoking technique.

Found on instructions for a fire extinguisher:

> 1. Carry to fire.

Or, if carrying it to the fire is too much trouble, simply start another fire closer to the extinguisher.

WARNING: Page 42

Found on plastic bottles of Mott's apple juice:

> Plastic Bottle. Excellent Source of Vitamin C.

To heck with oranges, other citric fruits, and vitamin supplements— eat just one plastic bottle a day and keep those colds away!

Found in the instructions of a Murray snow thrower:

> Do not use snow thrower on surfaces above ground level such as roofs of residences.

Anyone determined to haul a snowblower to the roof of a house has our permission to use it wherever they darn well please.

Found on the handle of a hammer:

CAUTION: Do not use this hammer to strike any solid object.

Such as, perhaps, the head of the idiot who came up with this warning in the first place?

Found on a butane lighter:

WARNING: Flame may cause fire.

Similarly, the water emitted from squirt guns may cause wetness.

Found on a box of light-sensitive photographic paper:

> Open only in total darkness.
> See further instructions inside.

*Let's hope those instructions
are in Braille.*

Found on soda vending machines:

WARNING! Never rock or tilt. Machine can fall over and cause serious injury or death. Vending machine will not dispense free product.

We have also discovered that you can't get any free milk by tipping over cows.

Factoid: Why the need for this warning? A 1995 report stated that since 1978, 37 people died and another 113 were injured rocking vending machines to get free soda or money from the machines. It is not known how many of those people were trying to buy Orange Crush.

Found on plastic bags used to protect newspapers from inclement weather:

> This bag is not a toy. Placing this bag over your head could result in suffocation.

Similarly, toys will not protect newspapers from the rain, and placing them on your head makes a really bad fashion statement.

Found on laundry instructions on a shirt made by HEET (Korea):

> **For best results: Wash in cold water separately, hang dry and iron with warm iron.**

For worst results: Drag behind car through puddles, tie to roof rack, and drive fast to dry.

Birth Control for Breakfast?

Newspapers recently reported a story of a lawsuit in New England brought by a woman against a manufacturer of contraceptive jelly.

It seems the young lady found the product came without clear instructions. She made some toast, spread the contraceptive jelly on it, and ate it. When she became pregnant, she sued the manufacturer.

We can only assume that in the future, the packaging of contraceptive jellies will include a warning similar to this:

> **WARNING:** This is not an oral contraceptive. Eating this product will not prevent pregnancy, has no nutritional value, tastes like wallpaper paste, and is not part of a complete breakfast.

Found on California Scents 100% pure natural nonaerosol citrus air freshener:

PRECAUTIONS: Not for personal consumption.
Use as instructed.

It was too hard to spread on toast, anyway.

WARNING: Page 52

Found on 24-ounce plastic bottles of Dr Pepper:

WARNING: Contents under pressure. Cap may blow off causing eye or other serious injury. Point away from face and people especially while opening.

Hard to believe the same warning label doesn't appear on handguns, land mines, and Mike Tyson.

Found in the instructions for a Hitachi HB-B201 bread machine:

> **WARNING:** Close supervision is necessary when bread machine is used by or near children.

The next page reads:

> **IMPORTANT SAFEGUARDS:** Keep the bread machine away from babies and children, as they may touch control buttons.

In other words, children can use the bread machine under close supervision— but only with their powers of telepathy.

WARNING: Page 54

Also found in a Hitachi HB-B201 bread machine manual:

CAUTION: Save these instructions.

Which is accompanied by the following explanatory note:

The word "caution" is used to indicate the presence of a hazard which will or can cause minor personal injury or property damage if the warning is ignored.

Does this mean personal injury or property damage will occur if the bread machine's instruction manual is discarded, misplaced, or made into an origami hat?

WARNING: Page 55

Found on a box of Trojan condoms:

> Any use of Trojan brand latex condoms for other than vaginal intercourse can increase the potential damage to the condom.

Using Trojan brand latex condoms for anything other than sex indicates that you don't quite understand this product.

Found on inside of cabinet door:

CAUTION: To avoid personal injury and damage to cabinet, do not move the cabinet while in a loaded condition.

Yeah, it's better to wait until you've sobered up.

WARNING: Page 57

Found on the packaging for a Ace garden hose nozzle:

WARNING: Do not spray water into an electrical outlet. Severe electrical shock could result.

How are ya supposed to clean out all that old electricity residue gunking up the outlets?

MR. BRILLIANT SEZ

Found on a package of sugarless Bubble Yum:

> Use of this product may be hazardous to your health.
> This product contains saccharin, which has been
> determined to cause cancer in laboratory animals.

Fillings now or chemotherapy later?

How'd they get
the rats to
chew gum?

MR. BRILLIANT SEZ

WARNING: Page 59

Found on a box of Just For Men hair coloring:

CAUTION: This product must not be used for dying eyelashes or eyebrows—to do so may cause blindness.

On the other hand, if you end up blinding yourself, you'll no longer be troubled by that gray hair.

Found on a package containing Gold Star Wraparound Safety Glasses:

WARNING FOR YOUR PROTECTION: This type
of protective product is not a substitute for using caution.

*And we were tempted to put on the safety glasses
and juggle chain saws.*

Found on a bottle of Brut aftershave lotion:

WARNING: Flammable until dry. Do not use when smoking or near fire, flame, or heat.

You spot an attractive person, you splash on a little aftershave, you light up a smoke for that sophisticated look, you—BOOM!— you spend the rest of the night in the burn unit.

Found on a bottle of Gatorade:

Scientifically formulated to taste best
when you need it most.

*In other words, if you're dying of thirst,
Gatorade tastes like Dom Pérignon.
Otherwise, it tastes like melted Jell-O.*

WARNING: Page 63

Found on a box of Equal sweetener with NutraSweet:

> ## Phenylketonurics: Contains phenylalanine.

Finally, a clear, concise, and simple warning we can all understand.

Factoid: Phenylketonurics are people who suffer from phenylketonuria (PKU), a disease that makes it difficult to metabolize phenylalanine, an amino acid found in aspartame (used in NutraSweet and Equal). Aspartame ingested by women with PKU during pregnancy can cause mental retardation in the unborn child. All products containing aspartame should spell out the dangers to phenylketonurics and also warn pregnant women to be tested for PKU before ingesting any food or drink containing aspartame. Also the FDA has concluded that experimental data "appear to suggest the possibility that aspartame . . . may contribute to the development of brain tumors." Why aren't these warnings on the side of a can of diet Coke? You don't suppose it would hurt sales, do you?

WARNING: Page 64

Found in a public restroom at rest stop along a Wisconsin highway:

Do not eat the urinal cakes.

Maybe they shouldn't make them look so much like cheese wheels.

Found on a package of Celebrity brand balloons:

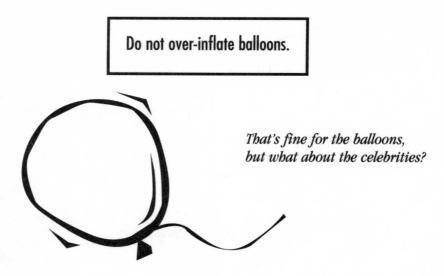

Do not over-inflate balloons.

*That's fine for the balloons,
but what about the celebrities?*

WARNING: Page 66

Found on white-pigmented KILZ Sealer, Primer, Stain-Blocker:

DANGER: Flammable. Harmful or fatal if swallowed.

With a name like KILZ, are any other warnings really necessary?

CAUTION: Bonus Section
Once Upon a Mattress

We've all seen the following warning on tags attached to mattresses, couches, and other large pieces of upholstered furniture:

> Do not remove tag under penalty of law.

Contrary to popular belief, removing the warning tag on a mattress will not bring a SWAT team swooping down on you. Then why is it there, and why so much threatening language over the possible removal of a label?

Furniture stores often use those tags to dupe unsuspecting customers into buying a damaged mattress. After they've accidentally damaged a mattress, warehouse employees simply sew the tags over tears in the upholstery so gullible customers, afraid to remove them, will not see the product's flaw and will sleep easier under the delusion that they paid a fair price for quality merchandise. Sweet dreams!

WARNING: Bonus Section

Found on a bottle of Scope mouthwash, which contains alcohol:

> Do not use in children under six years of age.
> Children over six should be supervised.

But a shot of mouthwash before bed really puts the kids to sleep in a hurry.

Found on a bottle of Mr. Bubble bubble-bath liquid:

CAUTION: Excessive use or prolonged exposure may cause irritation to skin and urinary tract.

We're disturbed that Mr. Bubble would expose himself for prolonged periods of time, and we're even more uncomfortable with the thought of him causing urinary tract problems.

Found on jar of Reese pitted cocktail olives:

Product may contain occasional pit fragment.

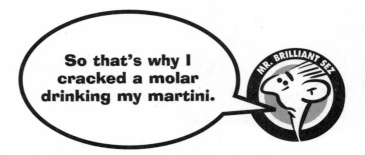

Found on a package of d-Con Mouse Prufe II mouse poison:

CAUTION: May be harmful or fatal if swallowed.

Isn't that the whole idea behind poison—that it's poisonous?

Found on Caribou coffee cup holders:

Caribou Coffee is always hot!

Dang! I ordered mine iced!

WARNING: Page 73

Seen over front doors of stores and restaurants across the U.S.:

This door to remain unlocked during business hours.

If your employees haven't grasped this concept, why did you hire them?

My business has nearly doubled since I've opened the doors to paying customers.

MR. BRILLIANT SEZ

Found in restaurant restrooms:

Employees must wash hands.

*Before or after unlocking
the front door?*

Found on a can of Ed Dwiggan's Private Stock Outside Semi-Gloss Latex Enamel lemon-scented paint:

CAUTION: Do not take internally.

Good thing Ed didn't go with the lemon-flavored paint.

And when you've finished painting, try one of Ed's new taste treats: the Latex Smoothie!

MR. BRILLIANT SEZ

Found on a can of Rave hair spray:

DANGER: Avoid spraying in eyes.

Looks like Andy Rooney is going to have to start using gel to keep those eyebrows in place.

Found on a package of Wellington twisted nylon twine:

CAUTION: Not recommended for use where personal
safety is involved.

*But it's the perfect twine for activities
involving the total disregard of personal safety.*

Found on a Northland jumbo size fire log:

CAUTION: Risk of fire.

Apparently the fireproof fire logs weren't selling very well.

Found on a Night Hawk carbon monoxide detector:

> **WARNING:** This device may not alarm at low carbon monoxide levels . . . OSHA has established that continuous exposure to levels of 50 ppm should not be exceeded in an 8-hour period. This detector has not been investigated by UL for carbon monoxide detection below 60 ppm.

Well, now, that should increase sales.

Found on bottles of Clorox bleach and many other household cleaning products:

> **WARNING:** Precautionary Statements: Hazards to human and domestic animals.

But perfectly safe for wild animals?

Found on a Wagner industrial heat gun:

WARNING: Do not use heat gun as a hair dryer.

Don King: Please read the warning label!

Found on instructions for folding up a portable baby carriage:

Step 1: Remove baby.

Baby? Oh my God! We forgot to put the baby in the baby carriage!

CAUTION: Bonus Section
Tipper Stickers

Besides cigarette cautions, perhaps no other warning label has garnered as much attention as those that now appear on many CDs and cassettes:

PARENTAL ADVISORY EXPLICIT LYRICS

The labels, dubbed "Tipper Stickers," were introduced in the mid-eighties after Tipper Gore's Parents' Music Resource Center argued before Congress for control over the content of music purchased by younger consumers. The

Recording Industry Association of America fought against them, insisting that government control of recorded music would open the floodgates of censorship.

A compromise was reached. Artists can record anything as long as warning labels are placed on albums with controversial lyrics. The stickers let parents know that an album contains lyrics they might not want their kids to hear.

But the labels remain controversial. Many retail stores refuse to stock albums carrying Tipper Stickers. And kids, experts argue, actually buy a CD because it has a parental advisory sticker.

Perhaps a better method is to place this sticker on every child at birth:

PARENTAL ADVISORY: Until this human being becomes an adult, he or she is your responsibility. Pay attention to what she or he watches on television, listens to on the stereo, sees at the movie theater, and reads. Don't expect the government or some cheesy sticker to do your parenting for you.

Found on a box containing a VCR:

Instructional video on hooking up your VCR included.

Need we say more?

Found in a hearing aids instruction booklet:

> **Never put your hearing aid or batteries in your mouth for any reason, as they can be accidentally swallowed.**

If your hearing aid ends up in your mouth, you'll probably want to take the dentures out of your ear.

Found on bottles of Excedrin:

ALCOHOL WARNING: If you generally consume 3 or more alcohol-containing drinks per day, you should consult your physician for advice on when and how you should take this product and other pain relievers.

If you're consuming more than three alcoholic drinks a day, you probably can't get the childproof cap off the bottle anyway.

Factoid: In November, 1997, the FDA called for new warnings for specific painkillers alerting users to potential liver damage or stomach problems when used with alcohol. The new labels will probably be easier to read after consuming three or more drinks.

WARNING: Page 88

Found on ACT II microwave popcorn:

CAUTION! Handle bag by top corners only. Open away from face. Bag and contents are very hot!

Unless, of course, you are using this bag of popcorn for a hot steam facial.

FACIALS:
Oatmeal, Mud or Hot Steam
(regular or butter flavored)

WARNING: Page 89

Found on GE halogen bulbs:

CAUTION: Halogen Bulbs operate at high temperatures and pressure and could shatter. Protect people and surroundings from hot flying fragments by using bulb in an enclosed fixture.

Is this a lightbulb or a grenade?

Hot Flying Fragments? Those guys at Hardees—what'll they think of next!

MR. BRILLIANT SEZ

Found in the *Microsoft Windows NT Work Station Basics and Installation Handbook*:

Do not export to Cuba, Iran, Iraq, Libya, North Korea, Syria, or Yugoslavia . . . [product should] not be used in the operation of nuclear facilities, aircraft navigation or communication systems, air traffic control, direct life support machines, or weapons systems.

*So, if you're hellbent on world domination,
do not use the Microsoft Windows NT work station.
Mr. Gates obviously wants to dominate the world
all by himself.*

WARNING: Page 91

Found on Mary Ellen's "For Those Days" Menstrual Stain Remover:

CAUTION: Irritant.

The last thing I want on "those days" is another irritant.

Found on Bowl Fresh Bathroom Freshener and Toilet Roll Holder:

CAUTION: Harmful if swallowed.
Call physician immediately.

We imagine swallowing any toilet-roll holder would be harmful.

Hey, Doc—I've got a toilet roll holder stuck in my throat! What should I do?

MR. BRILLIANT SEZ

Found on a package of Scotch electrical tape:

CAUTION: Turn off power before starting electrical work. This tape suitable for use at not more than 600V and at not more than 80°C (176°F).

Doing any electrical work at temperatures above 176°F really doesn't interest me anyway.

MR. BRILLIANT SEZ

WARNING: Page 94

Found on First Years Winnie the Pooh night-light:

WARNING: Risk of electrical shock. This product for adult use only.

Winnie the Pooh for adults only?
What do they make for the kids?
A night-light shaped like
Joe Camel?

Found on Sterno brand canned heat cooking fuel:

CAUTION: Flammable mixture. Keep away from children. Do not use near fire or flame.

How are you supposed to cook with a can of Sterno if you don't put a flame near it to light it in the first place?

What's the difference between flame and fire?

MR. BRILLIANT SEZ

An excerpt from the maximum strength Clearasil warning statement:

> This product may cause irritation characterized by redness, burning, itching, peeling, or possibly swelling.

So, getting rid of red, swelling, and scabbing blemishes means having to cope with redness, swelling, and peeling?

Found on Right Guard Sport deodorant:

WARNING: Intentional misuse by deliberately concentrating and inhaling contents may be harmful or fatal.

If you're intentionally inhaling spray deodorant, you're probably not reading warning labels with a clear head.

Why sniff aerosol deodorant when you can bake deodorant sticks into brownies?

MR. BRILLIANT SEZ

Found on Salix SST Saliva Tablets:

There was no warning label here—we were just amused that this product exists in the first place.

Found on alcoholic beverages in the U.S.:

GOVERNMENT WARNING:
1) According to the Surgeon General, women should not drink alcoholic beverages during pregnancy because of the risk of birth defects.
2) Consumption of alcoholic beverages impairs your ability to drive a car or operate machinery, and may cause health problems.

*Consumption may also impair your ability to speak coherently
and to discern whether members of the opposite sex
are genuinely attractive.*

Found on a bottle of Aussie Dewplex Leave-in Conditioner Plus Styler In One:

COMMON SENSE CAUTION:
Avoid getting in eyes.

Those of you without any shred of common sense
may go right ahead and attempt to condition your eyes.

A Call for More Scientific Truth in Product Warning Labels

As scientists and concerned citizens, Susan Hewitt and Edward Subitzky, noting that warning labels, however well-intentioned, merely scratch the surface in light of the findings of twentieth-century physics, propose more scientifically accurate warnings on the packaging of every product offered for sale in the United States of America. Their suggested list of warnings include:

HANDLE WITH EXTREME CARE: This product contains minute electrically charged particles moving at velocities in excess of five hundred million miles per hour.

THIS IS A 100% MATTER PRODUCT: In the unlikely event that this merchandise should contact antimatter in any form, a catastrophic explosion will result.

PLEASE NOTE: Some quantum physics theories suggest that when the consumer is not directly observing this product, it may cease to exist or will exist only in a vague and undetermined state.

IMPORTANT NOTICE TO PURCHASERS: The entire physical universe, including this product, may one day collapse back into an infinitesimally small space. Should another universe subsequently reemerge, the existence of this product in that universe cannot be guaranteed.

Found on Glade Plug-Ins Night-light Candle Scents:

CAUTION: Risk of electrical shock. This product is not a toy. It is for adult use only. . . . Keep out of children's reach.

So, to keep these night-lights out of children's reach, you'll have to rewire your house so all your electrical outlets are five feet off the ground.

Found on Intex queen-size air mattress:

WARNING: Use only under competent supervision.

"Not tonight, honey. We don't have a competent supervisor."

Found on KinderGuard child protection products:

CAUTION: This product is designed to help minimize accidents. Use of this product is not a substitute for adult supervision.

That's right. A television *is the proper substitute for adult supervision.*

WARNING: Page 106

Found on Weber gas grills:

CAUTION: Surface will be warm when in use.

*Let's hope it's more than warm
or these steaks won't be done for weeks!*

Found on a Werner Job-Master ladder:

WARNING: Do not stand on or above this rung.
You can lose your balance.

If they'd just
remove that rung,
they wouldn't have to
put a warning on it.

MR. BRILLIANT SEZ

Found on Superboggan toboggan:

WARNING: To avoid serious bodily injury—

- Do wear helmet at all times.
- Do use with only three riders.
- Do use while sitting upright facing ahead.
- Do not use while lying on stomach or back or while standing.
- Do hold onto handles at all times.
- Do keep entire body inside product at all times.
- Do wear clothing without strings or other items that may become entangled.
- Do not leave children unattended or unsupervised.

- Do not use near objects such as trees, bushes, stumps, rocks, branches, or man-made objects.

- Do not use on or near bumps, ruts, ice, or bare ground.

- Do not use on or near streets, roadways, driveways, or sidewalks.

- Do not pull using any motorized or nonmotorized vehicle. Only an adult should pull this product.

- Do not use when visibility is poor such as at night or during a storm.

- Do not use arms or legs to brake or steer this product. This product does not have brakes.

To ensure safety, discard product immediately.

WARNING: Page 110

Still not convinced warning labels are out of hand? Well, here's the mother of all cautionary statements, found on a flyer included with a Toastmaster toaster:

WARNING: A risk of fire and electrical shock exists in all electrical appliances and may cause personal injury or death.
IMPORTANT SAFEGUARDS: When using electrical appliances, basic safety precautions should always be followed to reduce the risk of fire, electric shock, and injury to persons, including the following:

- Do not touch hot surfaces. Use handles or knobs.

- To reduce the risk of electric shock, do not place any part of this toaster under water or other liquid.

- Close supervision is necessary when this appliance is used near children.

- Do not use appliance unattended.

- To reduce the risk of fire or electric shock, do not insert oversized foods, metal foil packages, or metal utensils into toaster. Remove all protective wrappings prior to placing in toaster

- Avoid using items with "runny" frosting, fillings, icings, or cheese. This includes pre-buttered foods. When these substances melt, they cause a sticky build-up and may result in a risk of fire.

- Use toaster in an open area with 4–6 inches air space above and on all sides for air circulation. A fire may occur if toaster is covered or touching flammable materials including curtains, draperies, towels, walls, and toaster covers, etc., while in operation.

WARNING: Page 112

- Do not attempt to dislodge food when toaster is plugged in. Should it be necessary to dislodge food, unplug the toaster and use only a wooden utensil.

- Unplug from outlet when not in use and before cleaning. Allow to cool before cleaning the appliance.

- Do not clean with metal scouring pads. Pieces can break off the pad and touch electrical parts creating a risk of electrical shock.

- Do not operate with a damaged cord or plug, or after the appliance malfunctions, or has been dropped or damaged in any manner.

- To reduce risk of injury, do not use accessory attachments.

- Do not use outdoors or while standing in a damp area.

- Do not let cord hang over edge of table or counter, or touch hot surfaces.

- Do not place on or near hot gas or electric burner, or in a heated oven.

- Do not use appliance except as intended.

- Failure to clean crumb tray may result in a risk of fire.

Sounds like it would be safer to vacation in Bosnia.

MR. BRILLIANT SEZ

So does that mean it's safe to stuff the toaster with toilet paper that's been soaked in lighter fluid?

WARNING: Page 114

And finally, the oddest warning we've found:

CAUTION!

May be harmful if inhaled. May cause irritation. Inhalation may cause irritation, coughing, and acute pneumoconiosis from overwhelming exposure to silica dust. May cause a rapidly developing pulmonary insufficiency, labored breathing, tachypnea and cyanosis followed by cor pulmonale and a short survival time. More frequently, after ten to twenty-five years exposure, labored breathing, dry cough, chest pain, decreased vital capacity, and diminished chest expansion may occur and progress to marked fatigue, extreme labored breathing and cyanosis, anorexia, cough with stringy mucous, pleauratic pain, and incapacity to work. Death may result from cardiac failure or destruction of lung tissue with resultant anorexia. Has caused tumorigenci effects in laboratory animals. Skin contact may cause irritation

WARNING: Page 115

and dermatitis. Eye contact may cause redness, irritation, and conjunctivitis. Target organs affected: Eyes, skin, and mucous membranes. Provide local exhaust ventilation and/or general dilution ventilation to meet published limits, or use of recommended NIOSH respirators listed in Material Safety Data Sheet.

Can you guess the product?
It's Washed Sea Sand!
Think of that the next time
you're planning a day at the beach.

WARNING: About the Authors

Joey Green is the best-selling author of over a dozen books, including *Polish Your Furniture With Panty Hose, Paint Your House With Powdered Milk, Wash Your Hair With Whipped Cream,* and *The Zen of Oz: Ten Spiritual Lessons from over the Rainbow.* A native of Miami, Florida, Joey now lives in Los Angeles, California.

Tim Nyberg and Tony Dierckins are the co-creators of the nationally best-selling *Duct Tape Book*(s) and the co-authors of *The WD-40 Book, When I'm an Old Man I'll Wear Mixed Plaids, Golf on the Tundra,* and other humor titles. Tim lives in his hometown of Shoreview, Minnesota, and has teamed up with Joey to write *The Bubble Wrap Book.* Tony, originally from St. Paul, Minnesota, now lives in Duluth, Minnesota, and is the author of *The Mosquito Book.*

WARNING: Thank You

Joey, Tim, and Tony would like to thank Dan Nyberg for the inspiration (your complimentary copy of this book is in the mail); our editor Jennifer Weis and her assistant, Kristen MacNamara, for throwing caution to the wind and publishing this warning book (despite our warning against doing so); and Ed Subitzky, Susan Hewitt, and the kind folks at Blackwell Scientific Publishing for giving us permission to reprint an excerpt from "A Call for More Scientific Truth in Product Warning Labels" from *The Journal of Irreproducible Results*.

If you enjoyed these warning labels, send us some that you've spotted!

Dept. JW—Warning Labels
St. Martin's Press
175 Fifth Avenue
New York, NY 10010

Or contact us via e-mail at our Web sites:
www.wackyuses.com or www.octane.com.

WARNING: You will not receive any money or credit if we use your submission in a future book. You may, however, receive the personal gratification of knowing you have contributed to a cause greater than us all.

CAUTION: Another Bonus Section

WARNING: The following pages contain REAL self-stick labels containing FAKE warnings. Peeling them off their backing sheet and placing them in locations of your own choosing can be interpreted by others as immature, impish, sophomoric behavior, and get you into trouble if you get caught. It can also be A LOT OF FUN!

WARNING:
This beverage is HOT! Allow to cool before spilling into your crotch.

WARNING:
Failure to lock this mailbox dramatically increases chances of receiving junk mail.

WARNING:
Placing wet socks in this dryer will result in the loss of at least one sock.

WARNING:
Failure to return this toilet seat to the "down" position may lead to marital disharmony.

WARNING: Shaking this carbonated beverage vigorously before opening may cause moisture in unwanted regions and could result in extra-fast depletion of product.

WARNING:
Opening this refrigerator door places your diet in extreme jeopardy.

WARNING:
Plugging in this telephone will cause telemarketers to call during dinner.

WARNING:
We have not made any effort to provide you with any warnings about the extreme dangers associated with this product. Use at your own risk.

WARNING:
Lighting this candle could result in fire.

WARNING:
Firing this gun could result in serious injury or death.

WARNING:
Driving this car severely increases the chances of becoming involved in a car accident.

WARNING:
Eating this ice cream too fast may result in "brain freeze" syndrome.

WARNING:

Failure to share use of this TV remote control can result in serious injury or death.

WARNING:

Misuse of this garment could cause serious social embarrassment. Please remember that this tie is designed as neckwear, not a bib or handkerchief.

WARNING:

Taking the last cupful from this office coffeepot without making a new pot will cause co-workers to despise you.

WARNING: Driving this recreational vehicle on a two-lane highway while towing a boat causes other drivers to curse your existence.

WARNING: Wear this kilt at your own risk. Manufacturer not responsible for sudden gusts of wind. Always keep knees together when seated.

WARNING: Striking the golf balls in this package with a golf club could result in a number of extreme emotional states, ranging from euphoria to anger and frustration. Do so at your own risk.

WARNING: This casserole may contain a hot dish prepared by your mother-in-law. Failure to enjoy it or to at least pretend to enjoy it may result in serious marital problems that will come up again and again.

WARNING:
This pencil could poke your eye out.

WARNING:
If you are driving a vehicle, please hang up this cell phone and pay attention!

WARNING:
This paper may cause paper cuts.

WARNING:
Three people are required to change this lightbulb.

WARNING: Placing a letter in this mailbox could lead to overworking a postal employee, causing him or her to become disgruntled and go on a shooting spree.